Dreamtime

AN ANTHOLOGY OF POEMS FOR THE EARTH

JOHN T RANKINE

INDIA • SINGAPORE • MALAYSIA

Copyright © John T Rankine 2023
All Rights Reserved.

ISBN 979-8-89066-755-7

This book has been published with all efforts taken to make the material error-free after the consent of the author. However, the author and the publisher do not assume and hereby disclaim any liability to any party for any loss, damage, or disruption caused by errors or omissions, whether such errors or omissions result from negligence, accident, or any other cause.

While every effort has been made to avoid any mistake or omission, this publication is being sold on the condition and understanding that neither the author nor the publishers or printers would be liable in any manner to any person by reason of any mistake or omission in this publication or for any action taken or omitted to be taken or advice rendered or accepted on the basis of this work. For any defect in printing or binding the publishers will be liable only to replace the defective copy by another copy of this work then available.

CONTENTS

INTRODUCTION TO DREAMTIME

This is an anthology of poetry for several reasons.

My first poem is Engineering 101, which went on in my life until the 2020s and as such, reflects not only a change in my style of writing but also an evolution in my own study and interests in both my life and my vision of the world around me.

My poetry was given a fillip when I read a reference to John Rankine in a book of verse by the Scottish Bard Robbie Burns and this is discussed in the section 'The Rankine Influence' on my poetry. Some sections of Burn's poems are included here.

I was an outdoor character in most ways, and this is reflected in my COSMOS poems. I was fascinated both with Quantum mechanics and all things Einstein, and also the concept of Entropy, which is reflected in my poems.

My bond and true association with the world and earth around me also began to mature when I began a landscaping business while still studying Botany and Ecology after my BSc in Chemistry and Mathematics. In 1982, I worked for 6 months with my Uncle Allan and Auntie Ruth, who were to hand back the mission land *in Yirrkala* in Arnhem land—a mission they had begun in 1951. This was the first time in Australian history this had happened and perhaps the stimulus for writing the poem, DREAMTIME.

Finally, this is an anthology because I have included several poems from good friends of mine: Jenny Saulwick and Prof. R.K Singh.

The fonts and scripts have some variation and this is in respect to both Jenny and Rodney Saulwick—Jenny as a community artist and designer and Rodney as a font and script designer.

This is an anthology of poetry and as such looks not only at various types and forms of poetry but also has used different fonts and scripts. This is not meant to be a homogeneous book of verse all of the same genre and all of the same author but a compilation of poetry that covers some 45 years in the making.

It is a work to be picked up and some sections read; it is not a novel to be read in one sitting. It may in fact need several readings to understand the influences that have imbued the poems at various times during my life—through my travels, my studies and my friends.

THE FRONT COVER

The front is a sketch of John Rankine—the author, made by the author from a mirror when he was 19—the age he began writing poetry and stories.

ACKNOWLEDGEMENTS

Dr. P.B. Saunders

Peter has been a continual font inspiration for most of my writing since my youth and my thanks for his additions to the final cover design.

Marie Therese Rankine

My mother was both my stalwart and my inspiration throughout my life, and it was mum aka Marie who took me off to Malvern Library and allowed me to read any book I wanted as long as I read. The poems in the final section refer to her.

Jenny Saulwick

Jenny was not just an inspiration to me over so many years but my muse when writing the script for **THE LOST WIND.** Just as importantly, Jenny was one of 3 co-designers for the amphitheatre which we later constructed with my students on the grounds of Selby Community House.

Tara Rankine

A special thanks must go to my daughter who has tirelessly supported me in not only this anthology but also all my other stories, plays and ventures.

Uncle Henry Rankine

Uncle Henry was the elder of the *Ngarrindjeri* people in South Australia in the area known as the RAUKAN Mission on the *Coorong.* Uncle Henry received some 10 awards for his work with young indigenous people; these awards included the Order of Australia from Prime Minister John Howard.

Henry Lawson

I did not realize the influence our great writer had on me as a young man until I included the poem 'From their Ivory Towers,' whichis a view I had of Prahran in Melbourne and the trams rolling by in a parade. It is not just this poem but Lawson's Social realism of his stories that left a huge impact on myself and my writing, which allowed me rein to write historical fiction or Social Realism which will become evident when reading my later stories. A giant of an Australian writer and historian.

THE RANKINE NAME AND INFLUENCE OF ITS HISTORY

The history and background of our family roots cannot be underestimated as we hail from Scotland, and this history has had a significant impact on both my life and my writing. One ancestor, John Rankine or Johnnie Rankine is alluded to in the works of the great Scottish bard and poet Laureate ***Robbie Burns*** in two of his poems.

1784 Epitaph to John Rankine

Ae day, as Death, that gruesome carl,
Was driving to the tither warl'
A mixtie-maxtie motley squad,
And mony a guilt-bespotted lad-
Black gowns of each denomination,
And thieves of every rank and station,
From him that wears the star and garter,
To him that wintles in a halter:
Ashamed himself to see the wretches,
He mutters, glowrin at the bitches,

"By God I'll not be seen behint them,
Nor 'mang the sp'ritual core present them,
Without, at least, ae honest man,
To grace this damn'd infernal clan!"

By Adamhill a glance he threw,
"Lord God!" quoth he, I have it now;
There's just the man I want, i' faith!"
And quickly stoppit Rankine's breath.

(Robbie Burns 1784)

1784 Epistle to John Rankine

O rough, rude, ready-witted Rankine,
The wale o' cocks for fun and drinking!
There's mony godly folks are thinkin,
Your dreams and tricks
Will send you, Korah like, a-sinkin
Straught to auld Nicks.
Ye hae saw mony cracks and cants,
And in your wicked, drunken rants,
Ye mak a devil o' the saunts,
An' fill them fou;
And then their failings, flaws an' wants,
Are a' seen thro'.......

(Robbie Burns 1784)

(the above passages are unredacted or altered texts of 18th-century Scottish/English and it should be noted that Robbie Burns has been the only Poet Laureate of Scotland. Therefore, do not alter any of this text or it will upset mony a Scotsman and Woman.)

These two poems sent me on an odyssey of search and discovery to disentangle the real John Rankine from history.

Much later, in 1864, another John Rankine departed Scotland and his Clan, with his young family, sailing from Portsmouth aboard the GRASSMERE to South Australia as a free man liege with a parcel of land and a grant to establish a settlement, or in this case, perhaps a Christian mission in the far-flung Coorong on the mouth of the Murray.

It travelled down the west coast of Africa and then along the Cape the Grasmere in the roaring forties to dispatch the family on or near the Coorong, and in the process, the ship broke the time record for the trip from England to Australia. The word Raukkan (*Rauwukung)* is translated from the ***Ngarrindjeri*** dialect as the '*ancient way*' and also '*meeting place for tribes.*'

These were Scottish Methodists and it seemed a part of their mission to establish some form of Christian mission. Then the eldest male of the family left after 4 years to settle somewhere else in Australia, and this is where my father John aka Jack Rankine was born in 1922 while back at RAUKKAN in 1922 *Henry Unaipon* (nephew to *David Unaipon* who features on the AUS $50 note) was born in the *Njarrandjerri* clan and several years later, Allan Rankine, my father's brother was born to be another Methodist minister.

Jack Rankine distinguished himself in World War II while Allan Rankine found God in the RAN and after the war, set up a mission in the far-flung reaches of NT in *Yirkalla* out of Gove and brought up his young family of 4 over the 2 stints of 4 years allocated to Methodist ministers. This same Uncle Allan as an initial minister in the Uniting Church was sent back to *Yirkalla* in the 1980s to hand the mission back to the *Gumatj* Indigenous people… the first time in Australian history that this had been done. I was there in 1982 to witness this event.

Meanwhile, back in S.A. at RAUKKAN, Henry Rankine was soon to be made the elder of the *Ngarrindjeri* tribe, and in his life was awarded some 10 Australian awards by the then Prime Minister John Howard; this included the Order of Australia for his work with indigenous people.

I visited Uncle Henry twice in the early nineties and realized when we looked at each other in the eyes for an eternity of time that there was a strong bond and connection between the both of us and the land beneath us.

I dedicate this anthology and the title poem to all of these Australians and am extremely proud to walk in their footsteps.

John W Rankine. B.Eng. Monash Uni. World War II. P.N.G.

Allan Rankine. RAN and Methodist and Uniting Church minister.

Henry Rankine. *Unaipon* and elder of the *Ngarrindjeri* nation.

Marie Therese Rankine. 1st woman on the Vic. Catholic Education Board.

Chapter 1

AN INSTANT IN THE HERE AND NOW 1975

A match thrown in the embers of a fire
flares then quickly dies.

A rosebud touched by the rays of Spring
bears its bloom
but then its petals quickly fly away.

And from her womb a woman bears a man
and in an instant, he wrinkles.
all his breath leaves him with a final sigh.

And all the instants are as much
As all the reasons are the same.

Thence we came and for just an
instant we are there
then gone forever.

DREAMTIME 1982

I.

I lie myself down in the sun
and listen to the river run
beside me
close my eyes
feel the warmth beneath me
find my soul
I am nodding
I am tree top moving
with the breeze my brother
my arms spread out
to anchor me my roots
growing into earth
my mother
my blood surges through
me into granite
ochre fusing my veins
into one

II.

I breathe and the earth
moves
the earth reaches up
embraces me
encompasses me
and we are one
I die into the earth
and the earth lives
see the river answer
watch the sun return
move the head so slowly
in the rhythm of the
universe
breathe the world and
hear the songs all
the absolute refrains
of the union of the sounds
of what we are.

PASTEL SHADES OF BEAUTY 1983

Before the blood light of sun
on the spinifex
picaninni shades of ochre
stand the test of time
as grass trees bear their spears
and come alive for a moment
in the desert scent
the days ascent burning
black bark and granite fire
shades of rock on the sand
colour of daylight breaks the
hills behind the mornings
opening of sifted sand.

Dew on rock
lizard on top of black crevice
chameleon changing colour
day changing light
spectrum through grain of sand
shrub becomes a hand in
the sharp half-light reaching
out of scattered arid land.
Twisting and turning
tortured mallee grey sinews
clawing at the milk of yellow
substance turned upon turn of centuries

Broken rock
desert stock
chasms become the chalice
of the deep soft green of
moss and burn into white lichen
leaves are green-bleached grey
bark is brown sacred blue
sky is black then white then crimson.

There is no more to ask but to breathe...
the charcoal of a fire buried in some
rocky crevice with fire sticks
the sound begins with paint and ochre
the deep hum of a didgeridoo begins
the stories of the hunt and the kangaroo
for this is the end of the start of a new
Beginning.

FRAGILE AS A MOUNTAINSIDE 1976

Fragile as a mountainside
in the mist in the morning
dropped down from the skies
like a single petal of a plant
nodding in the grass for centuries
as the sun rescued from the night
bleeds to death on the horizon.
So, the giddy path of a leaf in
the cold stream eddy...

like an old building wall of bricks
rising straight upwards to the rafters
on a windswept beach
the sands multiplying....
in the cities on the paths
the rain patters down so slowly.

Hear the rumble and the swirl
from the gutters
down drains storm flowing
tiles on the rooftops
red and dull and sodden
chimneys ever there and solid
watching
doors closed and stretching
white windows leaping into the night.
burnt is light
taut and strained...
is the crucible of life.

BRIEF GLIMPSES OF A NOMAD'S DAUGHTER 1994

Looking through my broken eyes of glass
I stumble over the dusty words of
past encounters...
Here is a letter written last year
to a friend in China.

There is a photo of a sacred cow...
with phosphorescent eyes waiting—
but not awaiting slaughter.

And then again brief glimpses
of my daughter's journey through
the looking glass
from cubby houses and hideaways
to fine brocades and different things
she cannot say or remember.

Some days are spent in wherewithal...
clasping at straws and painting thin air
it really doesn't matter where
the journey has the same
beginning in space
there sitting on the side of
the road smiling.

A SOFT QUIETNESS EASILY FOUND 1984

I tread softly like the cicadas
and quiver on the wind
my body in motion slowly
moving quietly forming my thoughts
hand comes down through thin
air and percussions the armchair
in measured softness
slow motioned cutting through space.
I tread softly on a thousand separate
gravel stones each attached to the other
I spread my weight
I spread my wings
and hover over my next thought
move I do like an angel
and sit before the stiff soft quiet.
for an instant I am the glass before me
crystallizing thoughts
spectrum of colour through wine
bending the light
evaporating like the dew to stillness
ever there behind the object
a feint hue of dust
on the surface of reality
for just a moment - I am one.

SYNERGISM (A EULOGY TO BLACKBERRY)

Its Battered hands form taunts
to the sun and laughs at blights.
its flower is simple-but potent-
plain but devilish cunning to survive-
grabbing my eye and knees
en passant says-it likes me-
in my attempts to be the master.
its fruit says-Come and eat me-
that I may spread over
more than your bread.

The birds from afar do just that
as they perch upon the branches
and warm their claws on the wires.
miles away from the plant to glower down
and shit my seed for my next family.
But the secrets of my plant are hidden
beneath the ground my roots and tubers
crawl ever forward like miners seeking gold.

While above my new shoots arc and lurch
in search of new land-an army on the move.
Fires and droughts are not a problem
for my genes are designed to seek water
enjoy me why you can and we will be friends.
use me and make your jams and fruit
topped pavlovas for I will survive....
our droughts and floods with my fruit
floating down the streams and perching
along your banks to start again.
Your barbed wire fences are roosts
to grow and for my blackbirds to
perch and eat my fruit.
So let us work together in Synergy.

We are different-but we are the same.
all of us wish to survive and claim
the broken land of banks and gullies
but the pestilence and herbicides we will
survive it all and still be there
with our difference but think of the
haven we give to our friends the foxes
and don't forget the rabbits and cats.

But let us work together and make a
different type of plant that gives all.
Graft onto it a delicate pure strain
which existence once before
was met with traps and poisons
especially prepared palliatives
but now its sap oozes into the veins
of the briar giving more reason to survive.

To rise above the grass with
full-blown pure-bred bloom.

This is the challenge that faces us all
the synergy of man and plant and people
from here and other lands to be different
yet be the same as one we must move together
to attempt to eradicate and tame difference
is a fool's desire to turn our back
on What has been here before and yet remains.
synergy is to blend and bend to our differences.

Take what you need and leave the rest
but never throw out difference
through fear of being coerced
we must simply encompass and embrace
those things which already exist
to make us stronger and part of this
land which has made men and women weep
together it is ours to keep for the long haul.

*(*epilogue 13)*

TREES OF THE OUTBACK 1982

1.

Oak in the morning breaking
Daylight has its destiny
of life before it mapped on
ocean masts and pillars
of strength that supports our dreams
of solid growth and structure.
We weaken with age it grows
hard and firms the stage beneath us
wear it away and it returns
to the earth to sprout
blotches of paint on a canvas
splatters of eucalypt grey
hue green leaves
iron bark that bleeds
and ire that burns fire.

2.

Black decomposing
womb of our life of
oil and coal and peat mould
folded into caverns
hover over chasms that
split then
slip away into the
boulder flung pits of bracken
firs and spruce surge to the heavens
box and willow anchor the
world together with ease
breathe the universe and
honey our birdsongs swaying
in the breeze
the balustrades of our existence
moan out their lives
in quiet persistence.

THE LEGEND OF THE TREE BURNING 1982

I.

The hand slips down into the
Afterlight from above
and beyond its feeble light red soft glow
stretching into the night a
long black shadow in state
flowing into that rigor mortis of sleep
forgetting remembering
slapped in the face by black
light of star shadows
heart beat repeating slowly.
Ha! Ha! The fire tells the legend
of the tree burning
each spark a silent dancing...
passage of time spent in long
since decomposing sunshine
or black lines of journey
etching into glowing eyes of coal
turning grains of sand into glass.
Soft shrill crack and still.

II.

Warm throwing out blowing leaves....
of the wind spirit arms
thundering carbon logs crashing
into atoms of crescendo
kettle drum birth of dust
rising up slowly
splattering the still warm
bones of Caesar's rust golden brown.
The sky takes a picture in
the still wasped fragrance
before the afterburn of
dawn hues out broken rocks from
long since slow combustion
tomorrow ashes resting in state of grey
forming glass mist gone away
funnelled down into cold spiral creation.

Acknowledgement to The Saulwicks and Gemco Theatre.

The font and script of the following poems have been altered and this is the contribution to the poems by my good friends Rodney and Jenny Saulwick. You may call me quaint or superstitious or even old fashioned with this, but every time I skim through these poems I think of these 2 good friends who were involved in so many projects with me that it would seem some travesty if I was to alter both the font and the script in these following poems.

Jenny especially would never forgive me. Our work together was not only concerning the script of the words, but in the appendix is a small sketch of the Amphitheatre at Selby house in the hills of Melbourne.

Jenny and myself were responsible for the design of this large Amphitheatre modelled on the small amphitheatres she oversaw the building of in the mountain ranges park.

That the Yarra Ranges Shire supported both this design project and that I was-with Jenny able to construct this large amphitheatre at the community house with my group of NRM (Natural Resource Management) is an achievement in itself.

That I received an art grant to perform my 2nd play:

THE LOST WIND

This play was performed in this amphitheatre with the help of David Greenaway and the Gemco group of actors must be remembered and recognized in this work.

Chapter 2 - URBAN DREAMTIME

WALKING ON BASS STRAIT 1988

There amongst the wires and cables
I sat entranced by the swift
sharp dives and glides
of the storm petrel
which, soaring till it touched the clouds
winged back again to skim the waves
black and angular prehistoric
it lay upon the ocean mirth
scorned the turnabout skidding water-
a part of and apart from me
it came so close I could see it looking
through me to another time
of still life paintings
sublimity tranquillity
I watched it take me away
from the steel decked floors
of man's passion to be
free It gloated as I stood and
stalked to the balustrades
and cried as I walked
my prison length across Bass Strait.

A NIGHT STORM IN TOORONGA RD

I.

Evening time brings a blessing over all...
and down some narrow street the road
reflects quicksilver in the distance.
tar splashed with white—
thrown from lights above as
water colours fade then disappear—
down black drains that groan
through grates then draw their loads
swell then spill their lots into swirling
courses careering deep beneath this earth
to meet surges in thick concrete pipes
spreading out branches that merge
then shoot towards the sea.
Dark within a blotched night
the sky slips down like a shutter...

II.

And right beneath
the light trips over gutter water
flinging out sprays of colour
in the afterlight
faced on either side all
along the paths that meet
deep straight blackened shafts
thrust upwards to receive and interlace
strong lines that weave and strum
fine network so to keep the street in bondage
rare sight glisten and hum.
See this wall before you
adance with a thousand fires—
as light filtered and bent through
a million raindrops beat against its face.
The wall again alive burning
as in the kiln countless bricks bleed the rain that
throws itself against its mass.
and then this sight is raised suspended—
a brand-new life is born...
while the rain waits to wash it all away.

SUPERMARKET DREAMTIME 2000

1.

This is the last offering of a super race
walking their mantra circles in their state
circumnavigating the golden valleys of waste
like cattle through the gates
they disappear into the night
without a trace
they are not walking proud wearing dilly bags
but lurching looking sad steering shopping trolleys
in between the burnt-out shelves
frozen mortuaries of suspended selves
the people look bemused, entranced
A sensualist experience dancing
with their four-wheeled recalcitrant companions
don't think of friends or lost maudlin lovers
think not of wine and laughs
nor communicate to others
make love to me now
clutch my full-blown plastic ersatz beauty.

11.

make love to me on the floor.
in the aisles
between the tim tams and the instant noodles
to the valium strains of times MUSAC
I am yours for the moment
with my perfumes and seductive clothing
I am yours for a price
wrapped in my own special
plastic sterility safe shopping
don't bargain but pretend.
Mine is the continuous stream of no time
the everlasting creams and cardboard signs
packs and stacks of neverending choices
such is the new consciousness of feel good time
the meditation in fluorescent light time
a walking contemplation of tiled floor
here in the whitey never never land
for the true believers in supermarket dreamtime.
We will pace the rows for aeons
in our glad rags and sad rags.

111.

till we are old and attached
to colostomy bags while
our next lives we are scheming
with plastic hearts and joints
armed with plastic cards
the beautiful 'how are you today'
lady fills our plastic bags
muttering our enlightened money mantras
this is our dreaming
We roll our eyes like blinds like
dollar signs for our new life preening
with our super
we have all our security under lights
only need to politely fight
for a place in the queue quickly, it's urgent now
we must chase one another for a spot
in the super race dreaming.
*(*See epilogue.1)*

YESTERDAY IN MY POCKET 2010

Looking at old photos in a box
lines you wrote when you
were not as old—
watch the embers grow cold
on one you once loved
smile at your reflection of eyes
in the mirror
count the people that have
died in your mind friends slip and
disappear on your sleeve
you have forgotten how to
grieve until you remember
old tired letters with young
dialogue written when you had
just begun to understand
tarnished cups won and found in surprise
eerie flights of Deja vu from a card and
pressed flower from a distant lover.

SUMMER WARMTH 1988

The road beneath me moves
and throbs its load of
black baked tar
zipped together with white
lines down to the sea.

And I see men leaning
slowly in the shade
dogs curled up and panting
in the dark glades of
trucks and cars

day slipping warmth—
sun spitting fire
to bake the bakelite on
the wires that shimmer song
and crackle like bacon in the pan.

the sky is aqua fire
and the people in the bar
are retarded with their
duty of imbibing summer

road boys burnt black
with smiles of dust and grime
young girls sleek brown
slide into the brine.
Pay day grows blisters in our pockets
as we incubate in slow
formed gardens with our friends.

We burn our feet on the
sand and seer our souls
in the evenings balmy search
for happiness and
cool soft arms of Summer.

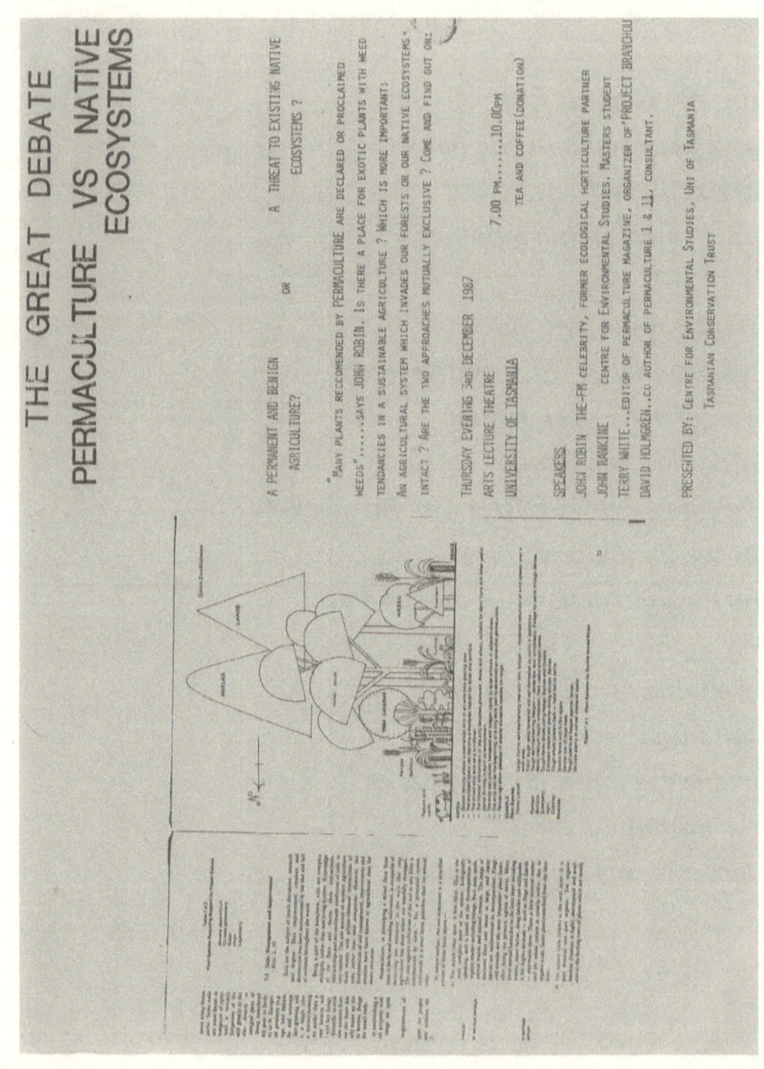

This debate was organized when I was studying at the University of Tasmania, Department of Environmental Studies in 1990. I invited 2 of the well-known exponents of revegetation and permaculture to debate with myself and David Robin, the future of our **Australian native ecosystems** and the notion of **Permaculture**: Here four of us discussed the effects of Permaculture on Native Ecosystems and featured some incredibly well-known Australians—all with their perspective on Australia's ecosystems.

It is difficult to know how much influence my work in bush restoration with the likes of Darcy Duggan (*may the native Aussie animals smile on his soul)* has had on my poetry, but this brochure of the debate is included to describe where my thoughts were in the 1980–2000s and still remains. This is my way of promoting this nexus of beliefs for any country. For **David Holmgren** it is The Permaculture Manual and many other publications.

The poem that follows: ***Walking on Bass Strait***, is both a reflection on the number of times ships bore convicts from England in the early part of the 1800s—but also the genesis of the Permaculture movement that began with Bill Mollison and David Holmgren at the University of Tasmania—plus the number of times I have made this crossing.

The four of us set about describing both the limitations and possibilities for the convergence of our native eco-systems and balancing this with the need for maintaining a sustainable agricultural system which could dovetail into a balance of the needs of both these essential parameters.

I know that so far in my lifetime, I have planted some 500,000 plants, mostly indigenous, and made all my students both here and in PRC plant 100 indigenous plants every year.

A DAY IN THE LIFE OF A WOMAN AND HERSELF 1978

Set the moon...
the cat has moaned too long.
And see
the child is crying.
so sweet though
when he sleeps.'
the streetlights are burning holes
in the glass before my eyes
the stars they have forgotten to fall...
have lost their way
in this ersatz model of a home with grass
while his father sleeps
will go away again and leave
me in my blessed misery of
a side street...
the world boils beneath...
It won't be long before he
Has his teeth...
But the day is here so soon
and see him smile and
cry for food
nothing more or less
than what we thought.'

And so, slowly, sadly
The sky has opened up now
With tears so much I could bawl
Where is my life amongst this wherewithal...'
Another day, another dream
and people curse and laugh
eave their lives at home
squirm through the long
day before the night.

> *'Oh how he laughs and squeals*
> *and crawls along the floor*
> *and stands and falls*
> *and stands and falls...'*

Between the sunbaked bricks and tiles
the road throbs and sighs and cries
mindless of the streets and
passersby whose thoughts are locked in
straight lines intent in their problems
tried, absorbed, disgourged.
Outside the women waiting
in the shade
trams rolling by in parade...
people rushing to their cradles
shuffling, sweating in facade.

Old men with fractured smiles
selling papers in the street
passed by, brooding girls smiling
moving sweetly
young men look at themselves
in windows scowling
Then look again.

All the cars are wheezing..
scuffling, groaning...
through their dreams
everyone is everywhere
pushing quietly for
elbowroom at the bar
choking in their own
miscontent.

> *...You will grow up big and smart*
> *And take a woman to your heart*
> *Then come to see your mother*
> *With children of your own*
> *But will she stay at home like me?*

Someplace somewhere
we all belong.
Set the sun......
This day has gone too long.

*(*epilogue 2)*

A BACKYARD IN GARDENVALE IN MIDSUMMER 1976

I.

In summer
the North wind whispers outside
out of breath
in through the windows
while the day takes its time in going
traffic down on the highway sounds
just like the sea
My body feels like a blowtorch.
while my arms cling to the table
sweat has seeped from me
all day and dried just NOW.
eyes-
my eyes ache into the evening and
yellow lights that have their
moths and mosquitoes
have disappeared.
Not one person talking
less energy than the old
fridge in the kitchen
hammering away

II.

The starlings noisily fight for
their beds and friends in the date-palm
another winter has blown
through my dreams
Christmas with its ironies and schemes
comes and goes like a weekend
which all these conversations held seem
hollow in the evening.
Hot air like bellows from
my nostrils
cicadas throb their noise in
the heat
like a heartbeat
outside in the car at night
travel to the country.
With windows open let
the wind sear your
face and scorch your ego
let the car breeze with
overheated ease
as the motor hums before
it screams

III.

Insects smash themselves
like flak
into the windscreen
sauntering through the
dim lit ghostly shimmering
comrades of trees
headlights are lead on my
eyes and lids
just a face waiting for me at night
two eyes to take me inside
two arms to hold my body tight
and the years and miles roll
themselves underneath me
playing nostalgia
before the first light of dawn
finds the spinifex.

REFLECTIONS ON THE VIEW FROM AN OPEN-AIR BATH AT COCKATOO

After the fashion show
the beauty harbours its master
slow flecked hair and dust
incense furious arbitrary discussion
feasts of nameless heads of state
are being retold...
distancing the lack of charm from
the charisma of cold
soft-headed enigmas
forget the hard seats and domed lights
the fragrant dreamtime
we have lost the key to the wind of doors
the special additives leave us
pale with moonlight
reflect the sweet smell of
the afterburn of dusk
the hue of dark carving
a soft shattering glass of stars
in a vortex of a universal vacuum
of nails and shavings

To look is to speak is
to dissolve into the green
black afternoon of dreams
I speak therefore I am
I am Oregon beams locked
together with spiders' webs
of threefold generations of
inspiration
The infinite is my space above me
the ocean depths lap about these
still warm jaws
sharks glide with grace and dignity
through the everlasting sea of stars
wading through the swamps of
the molten metal thoughts
of a true believer in time
I slip-I slide
I float in continuous sublime
this is the here and now
where is that bloody towel?

(epilogue 3)*

THE GARBAGE MAN COMETH 1988

I feel glee at the aftermath
before me
salt to the wounds of previous
living mirth in the
indeterminists of life's worth
slowly I pick up the remnants
of a civilization
slowly I put it in my pail
the music drones on to completion
I have no reason to be sad
There is no realm that
cannot be gleaned

The extant vegetation is disappearing
the philosophies of man are extinct
but I throw back in my
memory of wisdom
and collect the remblance once again
I miser the dribs and drabs
and collect them in a pile on my dustbin
yesterday's papers a denigration
of tomorrow's compilation
of facts of fiction
where were we? Oh yes
the garbage of creation
with me cometh.

Chapter 3: THE EARLY POEMS FROM MONASH UNIVERSITY

ENGINEERING 101 1969

Amid the noise
a normal day lets out
I gaze upon some
ugly smoking spout
which, like me
watches the day
pass through its phases
content
with its solemn task.
I move my head around
too lazy to move it
up from down
watch the clock's hands
struggling around its hidden eye
it too quietly follows through.
Off I go again
into some time-consuming thought
only to climb back again to see
that it alone has changed Not I.

WATER COLOURS 1976

I.

Evening time brings his blessing over all
and down some narrow streets
the road reflects pure silver in the distance
tar splashed with white
thrown from lights above as
water colours fade then disappear down
black drains that groan through grates
draw their loads and swell then spill
their lots into swirling courses
careering deep beneath this earth
to meet surges in thick concrete pipes
spreading out branches in patterns
that merge and shoot towards the sea.

II.

Dark within a blotched night
the sky slips down as a shutter
and right beneath
light trips over gutter water and
flings out splays of colour in the afterlight
faced on either side along the paths that meet
Struggling over logs
surging around mysterious obstacles
dragging shatters of light through
spectrum bends and noise of
roars and brown reflections
paper pieces, boards, shafts of
wooden throw-aways
like dismembered yachts hurtle tumbling,
surfacing for breath away from sight
calling back dimly
as in distance disappear.

BROKEN TOYS 1972

I.

What price a man to pay
these rules are almost
here to stay
to bow a head
to close an eye
and mock the mind with
lips so dry
a kinder fear
that guards the meek
so sleek it grows and
yet who knows
better than yourself
when life is life
and living is worth dying for.
what right a man to think
himself a man
whose mind is not his own
but broken toys
of boys
played with once again.

II.

We sit up straight
and sip our milk
cook our brains to
strain the juices and
lubricate the big machine.
Surely only one more
half an once
to test a tempered load.
Self-taught!
Self-paid!
Self-murdered Judases!
We struggle only with
our own desires
not hopes
Our hopes stay with the broken toys
and clutter mis forgotten
on the pile.
Borne into tomorrow
with yesterday's ideas.

FANTASY WOMAN 1974

Sometimes I feel so sad I could cry
so bad I could die
and then I close my eyes and
think of you with me laughing
beside me breathing
always hope and smiles
and warmth and moments
eternity could not tear apart.

So we are walking through the hills
with the sun so warm touching
through our fingers our hearts
we feel till our bodies disappear.
and all that remains is
eyes and smiles tide rushing upwards
surf molten behind
and above a million times faster
then gone, broken
the sky rains down in joy
as move we do like
angels to the evening.

OH YES 1971

My eyes are dying and
my brain is telling me
that it is time to see things
as they really are.
colour drops a shade
music colours even mottled grey
uneasy thoughts
ideas running stitches through my
seams
Tomorrow just another nonsense rhyme
Yesterdays added one by one to add
one more muted wrinkle to today
grown cold.
Hate just spat chips into the fire to kindle
Mothers spewing babies on a pyre to
mingle with the ashes of stone faces
and tiny traces
of what were once smiles and eyes
looking for the answers.

MORNING'S KISS 1981

Down white tight corridors
the angels move and glide
through the archway meeting
ragged breath
and smell of death in the
cocoon of sleep
wrapped in sheets the
murmur of life remains in
islands of resistance
quietly now and surely
through the dark hours behind
the dawn
they yawn and wait like
vultures
doing crosswords and writing
epitaphs to their lovers
fuse their days into
night
infuse the opiums
of dreams
to lost causes and bags of
bones.

I lie here now and hear
the dawn
I breathe and move my
way out of sleep
while next to me the
light breaks windows and
baptizes cold foreheads
daytime lifetime
nighttime-deathtime
and morning's kiss is
warm to me more now
as it is cold then to
the old man ex comrade
who breathes
his last
beside me.

Chapter 4: POEMS FROM THE COSMOS

INTRODUCTION TO POEMS FROM THE COSMOS

When I began writing poetry, I was still studying full time at Monash University in Chemistry and Maths and it was all about the war in Vietnam 1969–72 and my mother died during this period. So my poetry gave me some solace and escape from the realities of life, for though I had a girlfriend, the loss of our family home and mother at the same time imbued in me a sense of unbelonging and a strong desire to travel through the nether regions of Australia, first to absorb the outback and dwell in the living desert, which, with a simple rainfall came alive with all types of birds, lizards and animals and the memory of that amazing period in 1960 when, on returning from a car trip across to W.A. to meet up with our relatives, we became bogged in the middle of the nullabor and memory serves me well that we smeared mud over ourselves and pretended to be aboriginal boys and girls.

During my time in lectures and laboratory stints, the concept of Entropy reared its head and my imagination was enlivened with a wonderful understanding of the evolution and downfall of civilizations—that we were forever at war with one another in one way or another—blowing each other up or making yet another machine of mass destruction.

Our Chemistry lecturers were some of the best in Melbourne Don Gaff and others in physical chemistry awakened our minds to the notion of ENTROPY. The notion that a simple description of

Entropy was a simple car *chassis* rusting in an old field was simply entropy at work and Entropy summed it all up in some equations:

The state of disorder in the Universe and Einstein looking at black holes fueled my vivid imagination—for surely this could be discussed or explained in simple poetic terms that a layman could understand and so I tried to capture those simple equations in poems.

ENTROPY (From the Greek = change) represented by **S.**

dS = dqrev/T or DeltaS = S1 -S2 = S

And for Einstein it was even simpler in his well-known equation:

E = Mc2

If it was that simple why not describe it in poetry form?

EDEN BEFORE THE FALL 1980

1.

Light bent lines from above
flickered
splayed fingers of movement
played your arms in marionette
stroked your hair in silently
diffusing patterns
changing passions
passed before you.
breathed fire into your eyes
then roaring
merged all shades and sparks
of life to one sheer molten white
birth of desire.

11.

Suddenly,
like delicate master weaver
supple before the shuttle
re-arranged the threads
of fragile colour
into eternal tapestry
dancing molten movement
of brown and red and gold
subtle moulded features
of crafted ebony
are taken and then like bones
used for gambling,
cast into the pool
which shatters into spectrum.

111.

Then
were your smiles ripples
on the surface?
lips pressed hard and even
to a hidden shore
so, as you slowly
lift your eyes!
those black pools
lock within them past and death
and pain while the dull yellow spark
in their depths
smoulder on forever
keeps alive the mystery.

1V.

As now the sky breathes
fire in the darkness
so, as you slowly
lift your eyes.
those black pools lock
within them past and death
and pain
while the dull yellow spark
in their depths
smoulder on forever
keeps alive the mystery
and the future.

EIGHT MONTHS' RESEARCH AT PORT KEMBLA

1.

The sun heaves itself up from
beneath the waves strikes out webs of life
sparks veins in its eyes
that peer through girder and grate
imprisoned in this metal lacework
of burnt brown struts and pipes of pylons
bent brackets rivets angle iron—
then arching back upon the water
reaches, touches, glazes patterned sky
breathes life into this son of man
which shudders and seethes with ire.

11.

Bronzed giant supine
lying amongst ashes of smouldering sky
now belches evil grey perfume
through polished rows of perfect teeth claws at earth
rolls and crushes lurches and swings his
arms above him in circles, in patterns
scratches for his feed of coal and iron and fire.

111.

Our mighty warrior
we view him closely and see
the sweat pour down his native flanks.
So, he swelters in the midday sun.
as smelters heave and bellow
exude the sap from veins-
once trapped deep within the sands
and lands of granite.
Mud is blood beneath his feet-
left there in torn up no man's land.
To trickle and seep into stiff
Black lagoons
paint them brown and red and yellow
steeped in the blood of foe and warrior.
Running deep with the
mud of mother earth.

1V.

The morning tide brings in ships
that hover about him like
bees in a hive
bother over their queen.
bringing delicacies from
the northern province
and sweetmeats from
the western plains
These he grasps and he
clutches in
arms bulging
formed well in mutual need
he consumes and devours
raw with eyes closed.
roars with delight at
every morsel

V.

Beautiful manchild in his pen
moves quickly on hardened feet of
seared skin smooth joists
breathless elegance of motion
swings and weaves delicate strands.
fine strings wrought and stretched
tuned to sing praise
see him play strum with callused hand...
which takes sword mighty girder
and move through the act of war
pounds huge pylons with the ring of battle.

V1.

Ebb and flow grows movement,
slow swirls and eddies draw
out wisps of motion
past dock and ramp and shoulder
colder water soothing open wounds.
Beneath platforms and mighty boulders
on which perch men of iron
dusted red
embalmed in an immortal
frieze forever guardians
look and mutter across
at sightless slaves
smeared in black
and daubed with fire.

VII.

Generations of men beneath
generations of dust lifted from
coal loaders earth crushers
black and red, red and black
flank this stream of eternal schemes
and brackish plans
look and mutter across
at sightless slaves
smeared in black and daubed
with fire
generations of men beneath
generations of dust lifted from
coal loaders-earth crushers
black and red, red and black
flank this stream of eternal schemes
and Brackish plans.

*(epilogue * 4)*

MYSTERIALISM JULY 1997

I.

No longer scaremongers
only reality seekers
real life adjudicators
Forget the doomsday press
the idle thinkers
forgo the new myth of chance
the over value added
the kickboxing and line dancing
ours is the life of now
simple people.

II.

The new twin cabs shine
with their brief owners
behind the sun-glasses
black is the colour of style
or bereavement
for lost friends and
for holy dollars
that disappear.

III.

Surrounded by silent adulants
and disappointed dreamers
casino flashes glimpses
behind closed doors.
Another life and promise
a cathedral of chance
an enticement to open-eyed
believers
explosion of ethereal cash
burnt out dollars
slash and burn delusion.

IV.

For others who push
their own agenda
it does not matter
brief prattle and chatter
let us forget the past
and forgo the future
existentialism is dead
mysterialism is the true cause
of the here and now.

V.

Watch the glass glimmer
through a small square of wall
and door
push framed visions of our life
hidden within sharp angled blocks
of time
we look for answers but
our passion eludes
this simple request.

VI.

This is not the only dream of
the usanders
we have evolved earrings and
nose studs to deplore our
lack of sameness and more.
We allude to the expanding
universe
but hide behind our parochial lore
this is not change
but beautification of our
squandered past.

EAST OF ENTROPY WEST OF CIVILIZATION 1993

I.

Beneath a shroud of sulphur-laden dust
clouds of mist and haze smother
a silent long-lost valley
dim lights search for recognition
through the stillness
quiet clatters and shatters of
steel and glass
shards of past
disappear through the jagged
fabric cracks of the universe
like lost echoes
their plaintive calls meander
through the still black supra dawn
larger than life-long slow birds
call in passing from the hinterland
Away, away, away.

II.

Then
in the glimmer of the saffron
muddy, early morning light
plutonium-coloured leaves
rustle to extinction
in lifeless spasms amongst the gamma rays
neutron fractured sands
form then merge and take on substance
beginnings of colour. sentient rocks
unholy fallen gods of weary gold
sublime ancient centurions
petrified with dignity
dissolve into aeons of thought
Caesar's rust and bones and ashes
Revisited-re aligned
caught between the thin horizon line.

III.

Fronds meticulously matted patterns
hang abandoned in the cusp of caves
and claws of dragons
green blotches and daubs on
the landscape spill...
machine spun wires run their
lines and webs across the veltland...
exuding tentacles of sad warmth
soft sparks bright regalias
in the strontium stillness
mirages fly upon the wall as
shadows in a pane of glass
images of palm trees waft in the
haze of crystal grass
Cyprus shimmer with multitudes of
brazen insects in silver wings
their eyes glimmering with a million
neon colours of rainbow light
reflecting the previous yester aeon of
a one-day massive super sun
now a forever momentary black star
branches separate the calcium skies
eloping with the thin blue line
while...

IV.

Spiders plan a furtive
Reconnaissance into the steppes
in search of food and meaning
the hills flinging off their mantle
distancing with velvet grace
a bending of light through
the prism of night
some frozen murmuring stars
punch flecked holes in the cold stole
blanket of dark
scorched by the mandala
halo of the moon
Trees become smoke stalks
the pyre of dreams.

V.

Here simple themes slip
and pious ideas slide
into oblivion
stone mountains disappear
away into the soft
sculptured innocence of time
while snakes curl in circles and
touch each tail along the spiral
brooding shores of the delta
with chameleons and sand grass
growing up and
leaves and flowers closing down
the time warps of sharp
stars and faltering
hieroglyphics of eternity.

VI.

Another beginning reinventing day
threading together burnt out
microseconds which soar and
spiral into the warp of lost galaxies
tumble without thinking
back through black holes of past generations
gasses moving out and away
distancing themselves in an instant
from a centre of cold dreary atoms
exploding without sound
imploding where there is no flame
lizards fly in ecstasy and delicate rhythm amongst
scattered demons and dregs of savanna
above and through devolving
tablelands of frozen razor-sharp stone teeth
like sharks from the womb of liquid ice
consume the day timelessly
render apart the apache phantom
wafts of electrons lost unremembered
dismember the aquamarine
angry smiling Buddha nodding clouds
here chairs become tables become trees
with no thought of the future.

VII.

Then
from the grey whirlwind
and aqua streams of jet and
black and strange
acid wind and bitter rain
swirl across the Hinterland
brown clouds and wisps curl
together through the sometimes day
weary themselves into sodden fragments
clusters of tear-soaked sun focused ampoules
hang distended from a disappearing
branch of time leak and soak into
the sometimes clay which
full and stagnant
dispurges old cold world ashes
rust from Acheron
oozing sweetly its sour
course to Oberon and beyond
playing bitter jokes on the
few remaining stars and echelons
of super novas...
flinging the last handful of
entropy with trust at the
final plaster cast
model of the universe.

HISTORY OF THE YEAR DOT 1988

1.

In the beginning was the void the vacuum
where space did not belong
the no sound of voiceless beauty
black holes that would not disappear
flames in state frozen before
they began waiting without patience.

11.

In the beginning was the no time
of continuum and spirals of
forgotten fusion arcs of remorseless
ions and deep mysterious nuclear
dust of decomposing days.

111.

In the beginning was the no light
bouncing refracting and reflecting
the never never night
no prophets here nor gardens of dreams
just constant dry fission storms
The tantum ergo dreamtime.

1V.

In the beginning was the interspace
trigger of implosion—
framework of expanding relativity
gas roars exploding slowly fracturing
the lost brothers and sisters of
time's framework distancing the lonely ions
of the night and bringing to birth
the first chaotic iota of a second into eternity.

V.

In the beginning the first interminable
intercellular distance gave way to
overwhelming interstellar paths timeless
for just an instant—lost forever in the
juxtaposition—of tracer scars into nebulous
exuberant everlastingness.

VI.

Then there was the still and in a
moment another eternity in time
as bonds seize and fracture
matter is formed then dissolves-
All that is solid melts into air.

VII.

Then in the beginning was the slow fusion
as atoms and molecules began to be
flickering slow life forms
opportunizing the gasses and space and light
consuming decomposing being consumed,
again and again absorbing,
Disgorging deforming plastic elastic eternity.

VIII.

Then the greys became blue became
green became rules and associations
separation and demarcation
isolation and extinction of forms.
Still only a fractured microsecond in time
Devolving black macro stars and wormholes
As time itself began to bend itself
Around photons and ion streams
And with a final roar
The stars called out—
'Let the Universe Begin.'

AFTER THE RAIN FELL 2009

After the rain fell
They came in droves
Walking slowly trudging
With just glimpses of haunted faces
Beneath newspapers and Coloured umbrellas
But why is it they came?
Not for any quest or belief
Neither for enlightenment
But for only the inevitable
Slow glow walking alone
Bumping shoulders without care
With strangers.
A sudden fleeting intimacy of Chatter
Nonsense without regrets
No more forgetting Then belonging.
Under the patter clatter sky
the growl of slow motioned Delinquent trams
Garner their supporters -after the rains fell.

(epilogue 5)*

Chapter 5: POEMS WRITTEN BY FRIENDS

CONTRIBUTIONS OF POETRY FROM FRIENDS AND WRITERS

All poetry must have a beginning, and while I began writing soon after my mother died, it was not until my final year of my Science degree that I took on English as a subject. It was here that in a small reference, I discovered Robbie Burns, the only poet laureate of Scotland and the several poems he had written about my presumed ancestor John Rankine, inspiring me in my writing. Thus the description of a possible ancestor via poetry urged me forward—so it would be some dereliction of my ancestor not to include parts of his 2 poems dedicated to John Rankine.

Jenny Saulwick—my muse—and myself along with other designers at that stage from the hills and crew from Belgrave and Selby where we spent considerable time designing first, the ***amphitheatre*** at Selby Community house with a thanks for the grant from the Shire for enabling this to happen in the first place. But far more as we were able to take a group of 15 students on a work for the Government Program (NRM program) and actually construct this ***amphitheatre*** and it still remains. This was an opportunity for me to write and put on my second play with the help of David Greenaway, my friend and mentor. Together with the wonderful crew from **Gemco,** players were able to perform this play:

The Lost Wind

Performed over several weekends at the Selby amphitheatre during the summer of 2002–3. I have included not only three of **Jenny Saulwick's** poems: **CAPITALISM** and poems written by a friend and mentor of mine from India Prof. R.K. Singh, whom I have yet to meet, but whose work I have critiqued.

Capitalism 1981

I.

The spider knows its web.
every fly
        caught
        entombed
        waiting
to see what the spider will do
yet the mystery is
        it knows full well
yet it waits
being past
The blood of unsuspecting
Virgins know
not knowing
Willing or unwilling
shed not caring
Actions easily explained away.
        I am
        I will do.

Jenny Saulwick

II.

The mammoth walks at midnight
seeking that which will
        fulfill its greed
and the trees
        sentient
can only be trampled from its path.

Poems by Prof. R.K. Singh

R.K has developed his own unique form of poetry which is both universal and based in the poetry of Japan-**Haiku** and **Tanka**. The Haiku is a short artform in itself with some strict guidelines but still open for interpretation. The main aspect of this form is to Buddhist realisation and nature-which captures a moment in time and reflects elements of nature. It emanates from the strong Zen discipline of Japan and must fit a certain number of syllables often with often a hard-hitting message befitting the CO-VID pandemic lockdowns:

AGAINST THE WAVES

This is then followed by a stanza of TANKA which is also an ancient Japanese form of poetry normally categorised by 31 syllables but this form reflects the changing seasons, nature and desire. In R.K.'s case, this is brought home during the lockdown and the impact it had on human relationships and the test of love and desire. This often includes many literary devices such as personification and metaphor.

Prof R.K. has joined these 2 forms of Japanese culture and poetry and fused them into a style of his own with his form of three stanzas.

HAIKU

TANKA

HAIKU

Below are 2 simple examples taken from his anthology which I place side by side in an attempt to show the contrast of metre and metaphor, particularly in his emphasis on the seasonal changes matching often Christian festivals to those of Hindu ones.

AGAINST THE WAVES

Death of Desire.

Evening walk: a
Peep into my own
Lanes and bylines
Bodily harmony

A sense of inner calm
soon disturbed by TV
debates, news and
serials over sliced apple,
wholeness

before retiring swallow pills to
mitigate her rising hackles
that walk me through to death
of desire for love in bed.

There's no Third Day

Nestled between smog and dust
my church faces a collapse
beyond miracle: I can't
stand up to resurrection

there's no third day for my soul
no third eye for Shiva in me
God is too old to revive
the rhythm that was my once

I'm now defaced, mired in
scams constantly raped and
buried in chaos of abundance
Hope and unanswered prayers in
journey through crevice love
convulsions and faith shops.

CHPATER 6: POEMS FROM INDIA

My travels through India were incredibly formative, not only in my spirituality but in my poetry and understanding of the world's existence outside of Australia, and each of my five trips drew me back to the sub-continent, where I travelled to **Himachal Pradesh** to **Dharamshala; Uttar Pradesh** to the source of the **Ganges;** to the industrial business of **Bangalore** and its peaceful neighbour, **Mysore,** and further to **Mumbai** and beyond; **Calcutta** into a demonstration of one million people; and **Madras** and **Darjeeling,** always travelling by my bicycle and the magnificent rail system. Here I lived on dal and rice, chapattis and roti, masala dosas and naan, with freshly squeezed pineapple juice.

It was here in India I gave up my camera in preference to my pen with the realization that it was almost impossible to capture the beautiful chaos and beauty of India, but that it be written down. Thus began another journey into peace and simplicity as I began to realize this was the way India had been mellowed by numerous pens of holy men and women and scholars. For the very fabric of India is not the food or the chai or the holy cows, but indeed the interwoven combination of sights, smells and sounds of bells and song and dancing amongst the backdrop of jungle in Bengal and beyond.

DAWN IN THE PIN DROP SILENCE
BANGALORE 1994

In the beginning of the dark,
translucent dawn
when birds are ever still
the long caterwauling cry for
prayer searches out the faithful
invades strange dreams
invokes distant melancholy airs
slipping down snakes' scales
into aeons of coarse
cloth and pious rememberings
of eternity
the mosque invents the day
be still infidels and unbelievers!

Beneath the slow damp light arcs
the mist holds its breath...
smothers the still soft quiet...
blankets the slow-breathing dreamers
in the pin-drop silence.
Long before...
the cool burning feint shallow dawn
stirs to movement
the night lost shades of shattered
low borne landless vagabond colours
weaving through the streets
with nameless apparitions
baskets of herbs and freshly
picked frail sarongs
meander together
talking quietly jingling their bells
softly waking their friends
and blessing their foes.

So, the first drums soporific cry
is buried.
drowned by glares of sunlight
on golden teeth
challenged by blares of horns
Guests of Mammon and other gods of prey.

Here there is no sleep...
merely timelessness
for the urban ghosts, suburban myths—
plunging into headlong
pale aroma of incense
and burnt offerings.

The first crow warns in raven speak
disclosing shapes in closets
uncovers immaculate white clothing
moving with grace
searing, glimmering faces
like timeless scars along the road
quiet murmurs of menial random harvest
a whisper of mysterious chatter like
monkey breath
reborn the sighs and bless
the never never eyes.

The sudden passing of lowly beasts of burden
Quiet, disenfranchised of sleep
muttering in soulful eyes and moaning
as they eat their beds
of plastic bags and paper politics
they chew their leaders made of straw
tomorrows offering sanctifying
niches in the pavement
plants that agonise their existence
from crevices along the hunchbacked
stiletto ghetto side streets.
Sharks that hover above fast
disappearing mirages
call back fast sing song promises
waltzing and sideling past
shadows panel beating nails.
Hands moving and disappearing.
alchemists beating
burnishing brass into gold
breaking rocks into stones
turning stones into glass
then dust and ashes.

FROM THE EYES OF SEQUINED HORSES DEHLI 1994

I.

In these streets time is measured
in incense of dust
the paths are an hourglass
of scattered rubies of glass
and amorphisms
tired walls of ageless sandstone
with broken teeth of bricks.
Here
the kaleidoscope of
hallowed streams alive with
recycled mementos of Christianity
broken Empires favourite sons
the brief hurdy gurdy of
humanity
last messages lost in
coca cola bottles
brown, disguised as waste
nod quietly in adoration
robed in yesterday's politics,

II.

Slowly in newspaper print moving
retarded
sideways backwards
foreword
surging now chanting
with the crow and ibis
timeless martyrs to the
never ending flow of incarnations.
There on the now bright
regalia shore of shanty banks
evolves the glorious mayhem
of elegant squalor
children squat with ageless beauty
in the shimmering stark, parched
disappearing sands.

III.

Slowly- in the lost mirage of a
jagged dog snarled side street...
post suburban ghosts disappear.
Nighttime comes alive with
semi curves of human fusion
demigods of trucks and demons
screaming louder than the blare of trumpets
from bright lit temples
breaking their muscles and bonds
of caste
men by hand turning wheels of carts...
slowly mandala continuing
others dragging under straining loads
like diffident beasts of burden
while elephants in nonchalance
look down.

IV.

Saints in archways disappear...
like echoes in the multitude
stillness
doorways are holy passages of rite
dark framed meticulous
seclusion
packages of here bright
then gone now delusion.
colour brocades of broken down
disenfranchised noise
brick icons or palisades of history
scatter themselves
amongst the sandaled feet and dusky billboards
brailed calligraphy for steaming minds
in the quiet anonymity alive
dark eyes of faith murmur
with holy men in suits and beads
the jabber jabber Hindu dreams
of politics behind new jeans.

TO BE A BIRD IN DEHLI 1994

Sometimes it seems to me that
to be a bird in Delhi is the only answer
to living here with sanity.
They perch and make their nest
well away from the smog and the screech
and don't need to worry
about the cow shit and muddy feet
There are no traffic jams
where they come from
no shortage of food
the ever-changing piles beneath
are simply ready to go or just right.

Here is no shortage of straw
or paper or tinsel for their nests
especially the sparrows
that have created a new
housing estate in the bus shelters
no one seems to have told them
of India's population problem
they keep on laying eggs
they don't seem to concerned
about AIDS or hepatitis
yet they keep on drinking
that ever changing coloured water.

There seem to be no beggar birds
or birds trying to sell you things.
or shark birds
or Mother Therese birds
no stressed exam student type birds
and there seem not to be any
queues of impatient, noisy, running
late birds
or motor bike honking horn birds
or pushing, shoving, rushing
nasty type greedy naughty birds.
Just busy birds.

Maybe that's why there are
no haughty, wearing dark glasses
Mercedes driving politician type birds.
There are horny birds though
in Spring but they
always have clean clothes
they sit in the trees
in the breeze
away from the smells and
the flies and mosquitoes and
if they get bored then
they just perch on some cows back
and catch the insects and
the sun
the cows don't seem to mind.

Or if they go somewhere
they don't have to pay
extortionate prices for
plane tickets or
train tickets they
just fly away for holidays
especially the kites and hawks that
soar all day above...
the crowds like traffic monitors
chuckling to one another
and themselves
I wonder what they think of
us and our wonderful
civilization and often
think I—just what
horrible things we
all did in our past lives.

Chapter 7: A POEM FROM ENGLAND

SOMETIMES ANNIE IN ENGLAND
SEPTEMBER 2000

I.

Sometimes I dream I am in England
In the rain
Behind a pub
Near a bridge
Over a swollen waterway.
History and fist stories
Slap back at me
Old buildings cold mists
Hover about like the ghosts
Of laughing characters
who haunt the shadows
And forever stroll and clog the alleyways.
Here the timber mottles green
And grey
The stone castles lay and crumble
Old people grumble
About the old days
Before the Vikings came.

II.

So! the wind still whips and blows
With the lost and tumbled rolling
Stones
Along the causeways of the Mersey.
Sometimes I dream I am in London
Kicking out at puddles near Big Ben
Strolling round that bend in Piccadilly
Looking for you amongst the wall
Of strangers
Here the pavement buckles
Amongst the cobblestones
The sparrows mock the
Daytime traffic moans
Pigeon feeders scatter themselves
Like frozen icons
In the parks
And a loud-volumed green
The grass shimmers in the
Patchwork, sun broken clouds.

III.

Sometimes I see you there
Laughing with friends throwing
Stones that skimmer in the brown grey
Scudding waters of the Thames
I think I see your face amongst the
Clouds laughing down back up at me
They change and disappear
Like wil o' the wisps
Voyeurs of mystery
Then an old frumpish woman with a devilish
Smile grabs my hand and clasps my eyes
in hers
"read your fortune" she dares
"for a quid" and she does
"you are" she says "lost in time"

IV.

Sometimes I dream I am in England
In the frozen brown slush and snow
Battalions of blubbery red noses laugh
Frayed muted squawks from cabbies bark
And just before the drab musty day
turns to dark
mournful calls like lost cows
filter from the harbour
Then down Lands End
With the Druids at the Henge
And broken-down rocks
I see you once again
Disappear in your cloak into the black
Then fierce gaps appear in the cloud
I hear them mutter aloud
Soft in the rain that swirls around me
Well-travelled and surrounds me
This is the island
this is the prison for me
this is England by the Sea.

Chapter 8: POEMS FROM CHINA

INTRODUCTION TO CHINA POEMS

My introduction to China began in 1985 when as part of a conference on earth architecture, I had dinner with my partner in The Great Hall of the people.

My introduction to my teaching experience in China began in Kunming in Yunnan Province in 2003 where I began an English teacher experience that I will never forget. Those people and colleagues who knew me then will understand the nuance and references to these poems, but it was always going to be a halcyon experience as I arrived late for the beginning of my classes and was saved from approbation for the day I arrived was my birthday and was documented on CNN.

But it is the other lessons I learnt in only my first day on the job as I made my way up the stairwell of this School, I viewed posters that had been posted at intervals and the one that stays in my mind was a quote from a French Philosopher which I must share:

If you reach the age of 60 yrs. and look back and regret your past

Then you haven't lived your life.

I chuckled at this as I was still in my early 50's and had lived my life as if there was no time to waste. But while chuckling, I walked straight into the arms of a beautiful young Chinese woman who gave a large start and a big smile and politely said to me:

'*You are walking on the wrong side of the steps, you must look a\ out for yourself.*" Pointing to the next poster now directly opposite us that read:

SHOW YOUR CULTURE AND KEEP TO THE RIGHT

There was still much to learn and though I was forgiven my first day being late for class because it was my birthday, the warnings were quite clear from the start:

If you are late for class then you will be fined Yuan Y100

I was never late for my class unless I was laid up with an illness or even injury and this has followed me back to Australia and every other country I have visited, namely that I am never late for a class or an interview or a meeting. But there was much more to learn from China and I will leave you with my favourite Chinese proverb.

If you give a Chinese person an inch

They will give you back a foot.

A BRIEF HOMILY TO THE WISDOMS OF BUDDHISM

1. **AN END TO SUFFERING** (What Gautama did when he left the Jains in the sun and went to sit under the Bodhi tree.)
2. **COMPASSION** (This is shared with Hindu and other orders.) A feeling of empathy for all sentient beings. Why many Buddhists and Hindus are vegetarians?
3. **KARMA** (Shared by Hindus) Various interpretations. For me, you realize your own KARMA in your lifetime. This is not to do with re incarnation (Hindu difference) But Buddha said, 'You must strive to realise your own enlightenment in your own lifetime.'
4. **The concept of IMPERMANENCE**. Nothing is forever, everything dissolves into sand or dust including kings, regimes and mountains.
5. **NON-VIOLENCE.** This is definitely from the Vedic (Hindu) scripts. Think of Bapu. Mahatma Gandhi. Using this, he undid the British Raj in India.
6. **LETTING GO OF THE PAST**. Living in the now. In the present. Every day. Do not live in the past. Do not live in the future.
7. **DO NOT BELIEVE IN ME. BELIEVE IN YOURSELVES**. *(From the words of Gotama. The Buddha 551 B.C.) Gotama was a man and admitted it. Rather than believe in him we should all believe in ourselves.*
8. **LIVING BUDDHISM**. If there are three Buddhists talking, one of them will be a teacher and the other two will be students.
9. **HUMOUR.** You must be able to see the humour in all things. Laughing releases endorphins.
10. **LOVE.** You must be able to love yourself before you can truly love someone else. If you loathe yourself, it will flow onto your dealings with everyone else.

THE HAIKU LESSON

1

Fire hurts not once twice
On top never below ones
Heart until your Spring.

2

Leaf falls down in flight
Handshakes not breaks the sight
Will this begin another day
Or end the night.

3

Trees bear fruit not flies
Fresh-borne nectar tries to give
Sons beneath her Sun.

4

Hello good friends say
Goodbye to the wind
Then bless the earth.

5

Sharks have open lids
Kelp forests are dark brown cowl
Slithering many reefs

6

Will I wish life near
Here lie my pile of clothes strewn
Tomb awaits my bones later.

7

The wind blows the sand in eddies
I look down the funnel of this spout
And glimpse the mysteries of Eternity.

THE GREEK ALPHABET MEETS HAIKU LESSONS FROM A HAIKU STUDENT 2020

Alpha

eyes give us two tears
Some make us glad
Others give sad fears.

Beta

Fire hurts not once twice
On top never below ones
Heart till your spring.

Gamma

leaf falls down in autumn
Hand shakes not make trust flies
Will this break or die.

Delta

Trees bear fruit from blossom
Fresh born nectar tries to give
life beneath her sun.

Epsilon

Dreams come until they go
Myths, legends spirits flow
Achilles heel must take the blow.

Zeta

Above us lay the zodiac of planets-
No zephyr wind to tap our shoulder here
search a zenith of the cosmos for answers.

Eta

Turn up trumps not aces
Before four times rainbow call
Snaps cards under decks.

Theta

Sharks have open lids
Kelp forests are dark brown cowl
Slithering many reefs

Iota

The Beginning was just a void-
Only atoms of one moment an
Iota of a second past in one blast.

Kappa

Danger from the sea depths
Bereft of light but shades
Of life in the underworld.

Lambda

Last Sun drains the dark
In the crystal morning stark
Reminder of the midday sun.

Mu

Much more than leaves fall
Hair and rain must drift down
An eddy of time must whirl away.

Nu

Nothing is real except the leaf
That falls drifting back and forth
Past the horizon glimpse the sky.

CHi	Sigh the last sigh under the breath Of Sky above seize the last bud of youth And clasp it hungrily to your breast.
Omicron	Oh the sun rises from the east What magic awaits us this day before us Take it eagerly as there may be no more.
Pi	Death awaits us all Long before teeth exit fall But gums stay withal.
Rho	Brains trust body organs Fingers knees digits toes Nothing can remove a smile.
Sigma	Strike the bell Quasimodo Let the river to Oberon flow Along the Styx the boatman goes slowly.
Tau	Touch a person's face or graze a leaf With your finger draw a circle in the sand Glance at the orb the moon dip over the hill.

Upsilon	**Aeons of eons have gone before** **Between ageless epochs of time** **Long eras drift to dust and sand.**
Phi	**Will I wish life near** **Here lie my pile of clothes strewn** **Tomb awaits us soon.**
Chi	**Sigh the last sigh under the breath** **Of Sky above seize the last bud of youth** **And clasp it hungrily to your breast.**
Psi	**Live your life as full as you can** **If you have done well you remember** **If you have done nothing you forget.**
Omega	**Noire es noire is the final question** **Do we begin our life in black** **To close our eyes and finish it in Noire.**

ALL THE CROWS UNDER THE SUN ARE BLACK

In the summertime
all the birds test their wings
in the soft North wind
float and hover over updrafts
soaring down cliff faces
whisper out of breath
in the heat
just another hot blooded
heartbeat.

In the Autumn mists
These very same birds
Take no risks aloft in
The boughs amongst the gold
Turning leaves
Come down in pairs
Twos and threes.

So then the Springtime arrives
And with those autumn leaves
Build their nests in eaves
And hollows below the blusters in the sky.
Perched above the giddy flotsam
and jetsam of the seas and
brood over their young
They come down to feast on the
scattered treasures below.
They fly in circles and cry
and high their freedom calls
just singing their early morning ballads
search for, look for call for
one another.

They mimic the sounds of others,
Of young babies and lambs
And even ducks as they attempt to be
What they are not or could never be
For the crows, all the crows
Under the sun are black
burnt by the sun
They are black but not for
Want of trying.

ODE TO CHINA 2020

Walk down the plod
Of the worn trod
And exercise grief with passion
Here now the hard floors
And wooden doors and
Cries for compassion
You must do as we tell you
As we wish
You must never question
Must never be combative
Or competitive
Or too interrogative
Never on the front foot in motion
For we must do the interrogation
Accept this simple maxim of Marxism
For like the wheat you must
Bend with the grass in the wind
Not break like the oak in a storm
Warm to this and in the end
You will be our friend.

THE GENRE AND TECHNIQUE OF MY POETRY

Like many poets and writers, my style has evolved from my early days when I began to write poetry, which was strongly influenced, firstly by the death of my mother after a long battle with cancer and my introduction into Monash University at the ripe old age of 17. This is why I have included my first poem when I began Engineering and the thought still runs through my mind that while I did not know what I really wanted to do as a profession, that I would try to keep everyone happy with my choice. I would be an engineer to please my father who was an engineer, a teacher to please my mother who was a passionate teacher and introduce Cuisenaire into Sacre Coeur. That I would be an agricultural chemist.

Then, when I was an old man of 50 or 60, I would write about it all, my travels and adventures—and this is exactly what I have done.

As my poetry evolved, so did I, and my travels around the globe also had a significant influence on how I saw poetry as more than an expression of feeling, but also some form of travelogue of my journeys through life, while at the same time, calling on the legends and poetry of the past I had studied. Having studied for over 12 years with the Jesuits, I had what was called then and probably still is—a classical education.

It was here I discovered the wandering spirit of Ulysses to the Romans and *Virgil's Aeneid* which I studied in Latin and the *Odysseus* which I studied and sometimes failed in *Ancient Greek* but was forever absorbed and seduced by the sirens and mythological creatures of Homer's imagination. This from a man who was blind:

Two nights, two days, in the solid deep-sea swell

He drifted, many times awaiting death,

Until with shining ringlets in the East

The dawn confirmed a third day, breaking clear

Over a high and windless sea; and mounting

A rolling wave he caught a glimpse of land.

What a dear welcome thing life seems to children

Whose father, in the extremity, recovers

After some weakening and malignant illness… (*Book* 5 Homer)

Then there were other poets that left their indelible mark on both my conscious and subconscious thought and none more so than:

The Rubyaiyat of Omar Khayyam

which remains forever a strong teaching aid and my daughter's favourite. This is from one translation only.

The moving finger writes

And having writ moves on

And all your poetry and rhyme

Will not change it a single bit.

Again as I say this, who could forget the wonderful musical paeon or sage of *Beowulf* and his nemesis *Grendel:*

BEOWULF (author unknown)

Famed was this Beowulf far flew the boast of him

Son of Scyld, in the Scandian lands

So becomes it a youth to quit him well

    With his father's friends, by fee and gift,

That to find him aged, ion after days,

    Come warriors willing, should war draw nigh,

Liege man loyal: by lauded deeds

    Shall an earl have honour in every land.

(Translated from the ancient Norse)

It was not possible to capture India in a photo or with a camera as there is simply too much information and colour and visual noise to do this country justice. There was an epiphany moment for me in Bangalore, when I decided to use poetry as my eyes and describe those things around me in verse and hope this is more of a true representation of such a magnificent country. That I have been helped, nay... pushed by the giants of the past is my luck and a significant fillip to my humble attempts at descriptive verse.

Chapter 9: POEMS FROM LATER DAYS

EYES OF THE PAST

Too bad those wonderful eyes have
Gone down with the days
Their light is meaningful
The shine and gleam entrancing.
Not even words count for
The memories set firm in their depths
Their colour azure breaking down noise
Simply by looking they seek.
The wind blows her hair in a whirl
Around again and again
The dance is Spring says the birds
Clouds mumble 'we are here' they say
The wind grumbles to blow them away.
To await the sun is a mistake
Caught between two worlds
The day and the after night
Winter growls and bites at the tail
Spring is simply too fast.
Hark! Hark! Go the Cockatoos
Searching in the dusk
For home is not for all of them.

THE ALCHEMISTS

Woks and wooden spoons
Simple wands and tools for cooking,
but not Destruction
or fear or danger,
But they can be
If you get it wrong with the
Alchemy of the Kitchen.
My sister has finally found her alcove
and become a witch by working out
her Alchemy on the Stove.
By trying to poison me slowly
With this anarchic rite of passage
But has failed.
I am still alive.
Whilst my own cooking has gone perilously
close to derelict arcane.
The magpies eat my disasters with a determined elan
Munching on month-old fetta
with a less than delicate elegant delight.

Sage is much more wise and fussy
in a 20year old space of her own
climbing up fly wire doors
Eating, eating, eating everything
but my food!
Is this influence or inference.
The marinara mase-
The Greek salad passe-
Or the chicken thighs cooked impasse
Lemons are our only union of retreat.
And so We wonder why
We eat, we live, we die.

(epilogue 8)*

THE EGOTIST

Too many thoughts are lost at night
In dreams, whilst the morning lights
Bring echoes of the past but
We must never lose hope in lost
Despair
Black or White the future is the
Building block of thoughts that
Must stay-must remain.

Long-lost records of our life are
Reflected in the mirror of other people's visions
Projected
Sometimes we think we are never there
Lose hope and say I simply do not care.

But once beneath the Bodhi tree
Gautama looked around him at his friends
who had gathered there to worship him
as some God.
For he was burnt enough to look like one.

He shook his head and said:
End your suffering, get out of the sun.
'Do not believe in me,
Believe in yourself
Ego sum Veritatis.
Believe in your friends and love
But most of all it is yourselves
Who are looking for bliss
This life is the now, every moment
Then you must believe in yourselves
Ego Tist.'

(epilogue 9)*

EYES OF DROWNED SAILORS 2020

Watching from the boat on hire
Looking up on down with eyes and back on fire
There came to me a thought from olden days
Before the dusk, before the mire set in and
Grabbed me
Long before the night set in
How many sailors lay beneath me
In the dark depths of flights from decks
Burning, sinking with mast ablaze and jumping men
So, the crew stayed, but never men first
Into the boats
They stayed of course until the last.
Then I looked again beneath me more
For bones of old fishermen washed towards the shore
But they would be gone into the sand beneath
So, what did I see but glimpses and flashes
Never seen before   Nor never will it seem
They glanced up, down from the deeps
And in a flash, it was just a flash or glare
The eyes of drowned sailors
Looking up at my stare.

LIFE BEFORE APPLE 2021

There was life before apple
On our knees and desks
In the Garden
Of our choice
Amongst the trees.

FROM THEIR IVORY TOWERS 2020

The view from skywards down
Onto the streets and trams
Is muted here up amongst
The spires and steeples
Just a brief glimpse of
The melee of cars and trucks
And shouts and screams
Nothing but blue sky and the
Occasional bird that perches
Fluttering, then looks and flies away.

But this is nothing for those ensconced
In their airtight cocoons.
A swallows nest perhaps on a shelf
Somewhere, but here- it is silence
They sit in their dingy
Little office, while a stingy ray of
Sunlight flits feebly and faintly
Upon their desk below.

Sometimes they dream they are
In the country amongst friends
That knew them long ago.

But work beckons-another day
Another dollar
But still, there is always that perilous
Descent, by lift of course
To gasp some fresh but fetid air
Oozing from the dusky, dirty city that
Yearns for breath but we have
Air conditioners filtered air

A quick grab for something to eat then
Back again to repeat it all again.
Still, there is always the evening paper to grab
With one more glance at the life they have left
Far below, sawdust, sans cheek
Sans everything
But the weekly pay cheque.

**(epilogue 12)*

A LIFE OF PIROUETTES IN A GLASS CAGE

1.

Sleeping like an ink blot all day
now it is time to go to sleep
with my gut full of raisins and rice
embalmed in yesterday's misery
of creation.
I lie down with my wife my lover
wrap around me the walls
and I am the dark inside me
oozing out
and I stare out of this
bone-hardened, brain-tight cell
and scream inside this rigid
framework of mammoth architectural
achievement
hone my anger on straight,
bone chisel teeth.

11.

Every smile exposes my prison
bars and the force within me
bursts my chains and locks
me in a close red network of
blood filled stripes
my roadmap to freedom my
deliverance causes me tears
clutch my wife warm in my hands
firm and yielding
my fix my joint my whisky
my my my
why do the walls always slow
down just before dawn?
they are my own true source
of time my work of art.

111.

I am on the plains laughing
throwing rocks into the water
I smell the flowers and the
blowflies on my shit in the corner
hear the song of Beethoven and birds
and breakfast bells
I am here in body and soul
and mind and misery
clump clump clump...
down the corridor
of my memory
funnel of my freedom hides
this great door of
consciousness
breakfast plate a tombstone
on which I lie
bone idle.

(epilogue 7)*

Chapter 10: POEMS FROM A CATHOLIC CHILDHOOD

There are some 4–5 poems that reflect my time as a boy growing up with a Jesuit education riding my life and moulding my character as the Jesuits thought back in the 1960s:

Give me a boy until he is 12.
And I will give you the man.

I was sent home the first day at school in grade 3 for having my hair too short in what was then termed a crew cut, which really meant a number 3 or 4 zip cut and this by a Jesuit priest Father K who was bald... mostly. That I was and still am a left-handed person and found myself in an enclave of men who thought that left-handed people were sinister or in league with the evil powers was lost on my innocent mind of the time.

But I did all the Catholic things that my strictly Catholic mother and the Jesuits insisted I do and managed to survive the experience and despite many gain-sayers managed to graduate from year 12 and on to Monash University at the same time my mother passed away.

One of the poems then in this group:

'*Threaded together by Fine Gossamer*.' Is a last look at my mother from her bier in *Sacre Coeur*, the school for girls that she had taught at for all those years when my sisters attended the same school, making history of her own by being the first woman on the Catholic

Education Board along with my feared headmaster Father K from my primary school.

The other poems are a reflection of my time attending mass at St Joseph's Church in Malvern and is merely a reflective of my memories of the tedious process of a normal Sunday mass to a young boy of 12–13.

The last poem is a later-day observation of Christ on the cross and a question as to whether this was the true God or another poor soul who had been crucified 2000 years ago. Though the poems could be seen as a cynical reflection of a person who has eschewed the Church and looked back in reflection, it is also meant to show how early indoctrination can leave an indelible mark on the subconscious mind. My adoption of Buddhism and the teachings and ideas of Mahatma Gandhi, when I was first studying at Monash Uni, have lasted me through all these years and have not varied, as both a philosophy in Buddhism and the Vedic religion has remained with me.

MEA CULPA, MEA CULPA, MEA MAXIMA CULPA 1993

I.

I am lost in my reverie of a chair—
Splayed, buried in its
Suffocation
Crucified along long wooden strong arms.
I am lost in the reflection
Of past sins and recriminations
Of kneeling, kneeling and genuflecting
To the floor, the floor, the floor.
And I remember not believing
After lying in confession

Mea Culpa

II.

Yet I confess now to nothing except my guilt and
Believe only in my drunken spasms of
Inspiration
For in retrospect this is
My penance
My ungodly retribution.
Do we know of hell or have we all been there
Before the world began
I believe I have been told that heaven
Is no place for dreamers in my dreams—
For the devil is in us all
But especially me
Especially me, especially me.

Mea Culpa

III.

From a glance
The inner sanguine turmoil of that face
Reflects it all.
God in Venus the carpenter of planets
Angels crossing the denizen of stars
Apostles at the bar nodding
Slowly
Ave, Ave, Ave
Christ is on the dole—
Still
On the beach
Turning brown, growing old
Very slowly along with the grains
Of Caesar's ashes.

Mea Culpa

IV.

So I look to heaven and wonder are
These jewels
The Gabriel's, the saints
The celestial beings of testament or
Imploding, pulsating, dying
Martyrs to time
I search beyond the latest mystery of Wine
Somnambulist I wander, I seek
The journeyman, the sensualist
The decadence
My words and thoughts are everlasting threads of
Perhaps nothingness-

Mea culpa

V.

Moving on knees bleeding along roads
Hail Maria full of grace.
I bury my head in your sweet smelling arms
Fondle your soft, blue gown and smile
With intent
I believe, I believe, I believe—
In your chaste innocence, your firm
Breasts and thighs and eyes

I believe.

Mea Culpa

VI.

Is this ecstasy I feel a guilt?
A perversion
A drug induced addiction to confessions?
And why did I pray when I was
Drowning
Is this self-inflicted loneliness a passion?
A search for limbo
A lost holiness
I bury my head in my chalice of glass
And look through crystal into past
I beat my chest again mea culpa
I bless you my friends my enemies my lost
Innocence, without blasphemy.

Mea culpa, mea culpa

VII.

I am honest sometimes I am privileged
Other times I am not
Exploring the everlasting
Exploding the big bang in the garden of
Eden
Bliss in the morning
Multitudes of fish walking upon water
In the afternoons on Sunday
And bread with mould waiting
For hungry parishioners
Only the multitudes have gotten bigger
And eaten all the fishes

Mea culpa, mea culpa

VIII.

I believe and
Marx, why have you forsaken me?
With your cold frown and
Stilted blessings by decree
And contract
In nomine patris et filius
You have crossed yourself and your friends
And your enemies
With blood and water
Through the gates of the hereafter with
Newspaper cuttings and paper walls
Green tunics and red stars to Bethlehem
White nuns with blue faces
Ex comrades ecce, ecce, ecce

Mea culpa, mea culpa

IX.

I look at the thin, warm skin of bible and
Peacefully disembowel the lies of another
Age
Another stage of ingenious manipulation
in nomine patris
Beyond the bloody thumps of Yahweh
The swords the screams the banners
And cheque books of crusaders
Red crossed sons of jihad
et filius
Drawn and blessed and quartered in Brazil
Still Now it is better with bombs and gods
With cattle prods
But this is history, history, history
and will never repeat itself
Repeat itself

Mea culpa, mea culpa

X.

Dull
I quietly walk down the aisle with
Shoes making impious echoes off the high
Frozen walls of friezes
Mysteriously I scan in the stained
After light of glass
Watching men fall under crucifix of brass
Then it becomes clear as
I view the suffering, which embalms the walls
We are here so we must suffer also
mea culpa

X1.

The sore knees then on wooden pews
The putrid fish casserole on Fridays
The glory of broken arms in sport
People begging to be crucified for their sins
At Easter without nails
Then I see again him curse
See him speak in the holy light splattered
Shadows
Hey chum
Don't think I enjoy this
I just wish I were back in India
Smoking hashish with my mates
I wish, I wish, I wish
Oi veh
I wish I was a fish without
scales
This is your journey into everlasting
bliss
I am just the Jewish piano player.

Mea Culpa, Mea Culpa, Mea Maxima Culpa

PENNY GENUFLECT 1974

1.

Down the aisles they sometimes pass in style
Whilst outside the masses talk and congregate
The morning pushes close to noon
Should be almost could be seen.

11.

Down day's going
Down and genuflect
Of all those amongst us
The pious don't forget
In one day one second of an hour
The children of the poor don't neglect
And the penny tithe
Finds the plate.

111.

Last night's wine comes back
As penance
And the sun warms the very Soul
Nodding, down and praying
Almost halfway through
Mrs. B is wearing blue today-How daring, how dare she.

1V.

So, the priest rolls on in drones
Makes his point finally
And everyone sighs
Amen
Back to the stream
Flowing down the aisles
Communion, whilst children unattended
Make noise and aspirations.

V.

Someone at the back is leaving
People everywhere stirring
The sleeping, sleeping giant
Awake to genuflect
Cross themselves in retrospect
Eye Mrs. B's dress once
More
Then walk home to do the
Gardening.

THREADED TOGETHER BY FINE GOSSAMER 1971

I.

She was laid there
and stayed there uncomplaining
in her long black cocoon
with ivory hands
and the strong lines of morning
lashing themselves
to the willow.
Then she still aged
away from them in time
that kept about her
swaying men in unison...
around them fine gossamer
threaded by a delicate hand.

II.

Through those eyes gather
in the dusk
till some bloated sun emerges
merges with another
floats away
spread to nothing
on the distant line.

III.

Three bells ring in the entrance
of a holy man in the morning
dressed in absolute, blood red garments
the cruets of salvation in his hands
bends down in brotherhood and livelihood
mothers watching always from their hearts,
'O Deus'

Heads towards the floor, the floor, the floor,

'Veni ad Dominum'
The fine spirits raise themselves
their heads, like a storm,
'Veni ad Meum, Magister
Veni ad Meum, alecris.'

To them is come
through them is here
tumbles down this fissure
drawn by a vacuum
into the sea
of everlasting life.

IV.

I have gone away and left you
studiously reading someone else's writings,
slipped into another room
as the sun makes its way about you
yellows paper on the floor
turns an autumn brown
the colour of your hair
and you add veneer to the walls
with your thoughts
which wrapped within their womb
are laid there
and will stay there uncomplaining
till in the doorway the dawn
will find you,
feint hearted aspiration
return again
and miss it all once more.

(epilogue 11)*

EPILOGUE

An explanation of the background of some of my poems.

1* Supermarket Dreamtime

This was written during the 1980s when the notion of *Musak* was still permitted. This was played continuously throughout supermarkets both here and overseas, and it was argued that it removed annoying background noise in supermarkets, which it did. However, it also had the unfortunate effect of creating a semi-dream state, whereby people were not completely in charge of their shopping and tended to buy items they might not have otherwise bought, aka they spent more money than their budget allowed and bought items they did not really need.

It also changed the environment of supermarkets completely—from a place to catch up with friends and have a chat to a place dedicated to the God of mamon and spending. It was finally banned and removed from supermarkets around the world and the outcomes were quite amazing.

Supermarkets then became a social hive, and it was discovered that many burgeoning relationships were formed. That is quite simply, it became a new dating site!

This poem is therefore dedicated to all those relationships forged in post Musak supermarkets.

2* A Day in the Life of a Woman and Herself

This is really a story of isolation and loneliness for a woman with a baby and locked away in a suburban backstreet without support and without people to speak to except her new baby. Therefore, the poem becomes a silent conversation between a woman and her child, but in fact it is a conversation between a woman and herself, often exacerbated by post-natal depression.

This situation for young mothers was finally recognized and mother's groups and opportunities were made available for new mums to both socialize and discuss their needs and problems with both other mothers and professionals.

This poem is therefore dedicated to all those new mothers and to help them and show them that: They are never alone wherever they are and support groups are always available. That men now taking over a larger share of child rearing is also extremely significant.

This is also dedicated to my daughter whose upbringing and education was an extremely important part of both our relationship and growth.

3.* From an Outdoor Bath at Cockatoo

This is really a pastiche to the post-bushfire times in the Yarra Ranges and dealing with living in tents and caravans with the bath and hot water system outside. People who stayed over and wanted a bath had to deal with doing so under the sky or even better—under the stars.

4.* 8 Months' Research at Port Kembla

This poem is long and rather prosaic with a lot of symbolism and metaphor and describes a period of my life at Macquarie University in NSW during the early 1980s where I was researching microalgae as an indicator of pollution in an area known as Five Islands. This meant travelling to Port Kembla and working closely with other researchers at Wollongong University over the growth techniques for oceanic micro algae known as diatoms (in which I am still involved). It is the machines used in mining that I am describing as they began to take on a life of their own in their everyday work.

The difference between Chatswood and the Chase through which I cycled every day to the university.

5.* After the Rains Fell

This poem could simply relate to anyone in their youth who has ever gone to a Down to Earth Festival or Mind Body and Soul Festival or more importantly a rock concert or folk concert and it begins to rain and suddenly what began as an excellent idea and a lot of fun has now become a matter of keeping yourself and your belongings dry.

6.* A sketch of me teaching in Kunming. P.R.C

I thought I needed a balance with the ageing process and so included this sketch by a wonderful artist from the Forestry College S.W.F.C. in Kunming. This was an extremely wonderful and educational experience for me and a dream I had always had of teaching and working in China.

7. A Life of Pirouettes in a Glass Cage

I was recovering from tropical ulcers that had broken out in Northern Territory while on my way back from Queensland by car and found myself down on the Franklin Dam dispute in Tasmania in the rainforest. From there, it was a long trip to the hospital and a time I will never forget as this man was also in this hospital but was under 24-hour watch or observation for self-harm and everyone in this ward could see him pacing up and down and ripping at his hair with a look of total desperation and misunderstanding. It is perhaps the most harrowing sight I have seen in my life, and though it may not be a pleasant poem to read, it was both necessary and cathartic for me to write this poem.

8*. The Alchemists

This rather stupid poem was written when my sister Di and myself shared a house some time ago and had adventures in the kitchen with her special ideas for cooking. Mostly, the cooking was left to me, and this title reflects a short course I had written at the time titled 'The Alchemy of Cooking.' Though my cooking was satisfactory, it never really matched the cooking Christine and myself managed when we ran 'ORGANICS ON THE MOVE' throughout the East Coast and Tasmania. I dedicate this poem to my sister Di.

9. The Egotist

This poem is dedicated to my other sister Jacq, who for many years simply referred to me as being *so egotistical.* Which I am! But there is room for being unselfish and supporting other people and time to devote to your own study and work. It is true that sometimes it is difficult to find a balance and one's own ambitions and interests can take over and consume your other duties which seemed not to be a problem in earlier times. But life is short, however long we live, and looking for some balance is what this poem is meant to be about.

10. The Never Never

This poem is a double entendre on the term *The Never Never.* It is a term that relates to an expression for the Australian outback. The saying went 'You *never never want to go there— 'cause you never ever come back!'*

This was true for a number of early explorers in Australia and still has its warning note. It also refers to finality, and this poem is meant as *a in memorium* to a student who was writing a final exam in Maths in the Great Hall, and though I knew I had failed the exam and shook my head, the young woman went hysterical and was escorted from the hall with no follow-up counselling. She took herself to the top floor of the Ming Wing and threw herself off the top of the building. We formed a group to put a submission to the administration to ensure all future science exams were to be assessed by mid-year exams, tutorial sheets and questions, and in the case of Chemistry and Physics students also allowing for practical reports rather than a single end-of-year exam. This was adopted for all future assessments by the administration. However, it also had an impact on others, including my daughter, as a friend of hers who took the same approach to life and expectations that often are forced upon them by parents.

This simple poem is dedicated to students all over the world who find that their studies have pushed them to the wall and that there is always a future chance to take exams and perhaps even use it as a time to reflect on their own choice as to their future career.

11.* Threaded together by fine gossamer

This poem was written a long while after my mother had passed away from a long battle with cancer and is really the hollowness we all felt at her funeral at the Sacre Coeur Chapel. That we all were totally gutted and worn out by the experience which left us all bereft of tears, as most people would relate to, and a loss that could never be replaced. At that age, mothers are not replaceable.

12.* From their ivory towers

The second verse has a section that relates to Henry Lawson's poem which was inadvertent but seems to sum up the period of time when I was dealing with two legal firms, both based on the top floor and somewhere in Melbourne city.

My apologies to Henry Lawson if this is the case, but the stanza, though it is more than a century old, sums up the alienation of people in a big city. I must give ***Henry Lawson*** the credit for inspiring me in his view of the outback and having the skill to turn these observations into verse. I am a simple student of his work and it has flown from my memory. I have not removed it from the poem, but dedicate some of the influences of my poetry to the Aussie Bard-Henry Lawson.

13. *Synergism (A eulogy to Blackberry)

This is a more of a testament to the influence that Blackberry (Rubus fruticosos. L agg) has played in my life as I attempted to find a way of using weeds as colonizing spp. And thus a means for re-vegetation of indigenous plants. While this worked to some degree, it was definitely made work by David Holmgren on his property especially in gullies where Blackberries flourished. My intent in the debate in Tasmania '**The Great Debate**' was to come to terms with the balance required in exotic plants which make up the majority of our vegetable intake and pasture species and the need to continue to preserve our native vegetation and ecosystems which was the basis of John Robin's work with his business 'Ecological Horticulture.'

However, it turned into a love hate relationship between me and the blackberries as this was the basis of an MSc at Monash University and the role blackberry could play in the role of plant succession.

In the research into weeds and colonizing species, I found that the best primary colonizer for any area around the world is common bracken and its sub species. That I contacted numerous people in the field concerning a range of weeds and the possibility, it was a researcher in New Zealand that found it quite possible to use this technique in controlling Gorse (*Ulex Europaeus*) in pastureland and the Gorse acted as a nursery plant to stop grazing by the local cattle and sheep.

There is no question that the concept of colonization by so called weed species and then the introduction of indigenous vegetation is a way forward now in large scale- or small-scale revegetation programs.

This is specifically true of bracken fern which was the first plant to return after the volcanic eruption on Krakatoa in 1883 as the primary colonizing species.

Though the poem might be a bad example of verse, it is an attempt to explain the view that many people in the industry regard many plants as weeds and the only method to control them is to use herbicides. However, if these plants are considered as healers of a broken land and colonizing species for future regeneration, then large tracts of land could be regenerated and the 'weed' problem would cease to be a problem. I am hoping to make this issue and the evolution of agriculture, the basis of a future text book.)

WORKS OF WRITING OR PLAYS YET TO COME

RATTUS RATTUS

The following are songs taken from my play ***RATTUS RATTUS***, a dialectic play where I look at the way people view animals—in this case, RATS and how animals view humans and cats. In this case, the rats become the protagonists and the cat becomes the antagonists. The underdogs (rats) become the heroes of this story. While this play is being turned into a book, there is still the option of producing this play—with strong reference to the modus of Bollywood.

—My thanks and apologies to our brave Aussie *Desert Rats* from Tobruk.

STRANGE TALES from the SEA

This is a book of short stories set on or about the ocean that covers episodes of the Rankine's journeying to S.A. on the Grasmere in 1863—the ship breaking the speed record from the U.K. to S.A. along the way, thanks to a great ship and an intrepid crew and captain. This is only the beginning of a journey that takes the entire Rankine clan through the Second World War over various oceans and waterways. It also includes true stories of mishaps and close calls which seemed to mirror the life of the Rankine clan who spent a large amount of time either on the waves, being swept off the rocks to their death, or under the ocean with sharks and stingrays. This is a cross-generational series of stories that bring in the women of various families into the face of the waves and dangers of the shipwreck coast, and beyond.

The Lost Wind

The following diagram is a representation of the amphitheatre which was co-designed with Jenny Saulwick and Iain Milne as a part of the AECOS Team. This was presented to the Shire of Yarra Ranges and was constructed as a part of an NRM project employing some 15 young people. The amphitheatre was completed in 2003 and the play **THE LOST WIND** (John Rankine) was performed here over the month of March 2003 in this amphitheatre with a grant from the Arts Council.

THE AMPHITHEATRE AT SELBY VICTORIA

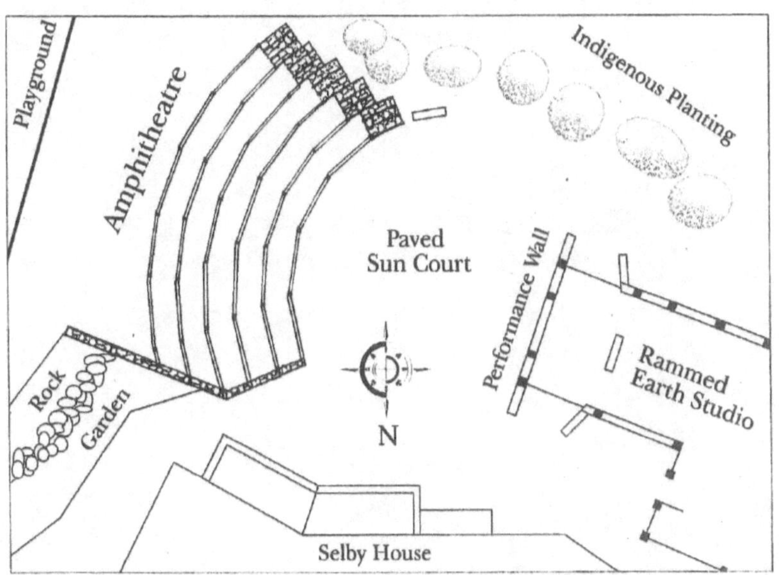

www.ingramcontent.com/pod-product-compliance
Lightning Source LLC
LaVergne TN
LVHW091047150826
845673LV00002B/487

* 9 7 9 8 8 9 0 6 6 7 5 5 7 *